the trouble with sti

The Trouble With Stitches

sean o huigin

Black Moss Press

Published by Black Moss Press, p.o. box 143, Station A, Windsor, Ontario. Acknowledgement for financial assistance towards publication is due both the Canada Council and the Ontario Arts Council.

Distributed by Firefly Books, 3520 Pharmacy Avenue, Unit 1C, Scarborough, Ontario.

Typeset in Bodoni by The Coach House Press (Toronto), printed and bound by The Porcupine's Quill (Erin). The stock is Zephyr laid.

Illustrations by Anthony LeBaron.

ISBN 0-88753-078-8

this book is dedicated to Walter Sinclair

would you

i would
would you
i certainly
would
i wonder if
you would
why would
you
well
in that case
i suppose
i would
too
.

the measles

the measles
the measles
are coming
EEEEEEK
they're
already here
they're on
my chest and
all the rest
stare back at
me from the
mirror
my face has
spots and i
feel all hot
and i wish
they would
disappear
'cause i'm
stuck in
bed with a
spotty head
and my friends
aren't allowed
to come near

i moan and
groan when
i'm stuck at
home and
i drive my
mother mad
when the
spots are
gone and my
clear skin's
on
boy will she
be glad
.

the trouble with stitches

the trouble
with having
stitches
is that it
really itches
as they
heal
you get them
in all sorts
of ways
on rainy or
on sunny
days
by falling
or by getting
hit
so many ways
your skin
can split
and OW
OH WOW
you get them
on your arm or
head
they come from
falling out
of bed

on legs and
feet they're
sometimes
needed
anywhere you might
have bleeded
the doctor has
to put them in
with needles
not a safety pin
you often get
a bandage too
there is no
extra charge to you
for that
and then
you have to go
again
a week or two
or maybe three
later so the doc
can see
the bits of thread
and take them out
it doesn't hurt
no need to
shout

they sometimes
go away themselves
perhaps that's
done by little
elves
at any rate
in any
weather
now your skin
will hold
together
.

the big orange wonder

i saw a big
orange plane today
coming down to
land from a pale
blue sky
and it made me
wonder

do orange planes
run on orange juice
instead of airplane
fuel
do the airhostesses
wear orange uniforms
and serve you meals
of carrots and
turnip with orange
ice cream for dessert

do they give you
orange pop to drink
and maybe give your
mother some orange
nailpolish for
a present and even
give you an orange
balloon

do the pilots
wear orange underwear
and do you buy your ticket
at an orange counter
from a man with
freckles and orange eyes

i wonder
i wonder
.

oh oh!

have you ever
been in
a car
or on a bus
or out somewhere
or walking down
the street and
suddenly
you have to
pee
oh wow
there's nowhere
to go
no bathroom
no bushes
no place you
can get
behind
and it's
getting worse

there's nothing
to do
but wait
and hope
and cross
your fingers
and your legs
and curl up
your toes
and bounce a bit
from foot to
foot
or sit very
still and
hope you don't
hit any bumps

and there's not
a thing
your mother
can do
or your father
and you feel like
you're going
to burst

well
i think
everybody
should carry
a milk jug
and wear a
very long
baggy coat
just in case
.

i've got a cold

'i've got a cold'
said Mary
'and it is very
very
unpleasant
'cause my nose
drips down
and my head
stuffs up
so i have a cup
of tea and i
drink it down

i nibble on
garlic
i swallow
an onion
i eat lots of
chili peppers
too
but my nose
gets red on
my stuffed up
head and
i hope it
doesn't happen
to you

i rub on Vicks
and i take some
pills and i
suck on some
cough candies
with the juice
of a lemon
i look up to
heaven and
i pray on my
bended knees

but the cold
stays on
and my nose
still drips
and my teeth
even start to
ache
so i go to bed
with my stuffed
up head
i lie there
wide awake

it's hard
to breathe
and i sure can't
sleep and
my chest's
getting stuffed
up good
mom brings
some soup
and some medicine
and i take
all the things
i should

but it's all
no use
and i feel so
bad and
i sniffle and
i snuffle and
i whine

for the only
thing that will
cure this cold
is a good long
dose of
time'
.

this is a poem

this is a poem
for people who
stand
they stand very
straight
and hold up
their hands
like me
like me
pretend that
you are a tree

this is a poem
for people who
wave
they wave to
the front
and then make
a cave
with their arms
their arms
a cave made of
wrapped around
arms

this is a poem
for people who
blink
they blink both
their eyes
and then they
can wink
each one
each one
and giggle when
they are done

this is a poem
for people who
sleep
they drop down
their head
and breathe very
deep
and they snore
they snore
and then they
do it once more

this is a poem
for people who
bend
they bend at
the middle and
tickle the end
of their toe
their toe
they have to
do it just so

this is a poem
for people who
fly
they flap at
the arms and
i wonder why
they do
they do
i'm telling you
they really do

this is a poem
you might
find in your pocket
bring it out
and pretend it's
a locket
to wear 'round
your neck
like this
like this
and now you must
throw me
a kiss

this is a poem
to hold in
the air
you wave it
around and
point over there
you do
you do
you'll see that
i do it too

this is a poem
to read when
you sit
and that of
course is the
end of it

.

the tooth

i have a tooth
thatth very looth
i think itth coming
out
my dad had one
and we had fun
thearching all
about
you thee he tied
a thtring to it
and one end to
the door
and got my mom
to thlam it
hard
the tooth fell
on the floor
he thaid
whoever found
it
could put it
underneath
their pillow and
the tooth fairy
would leave
a dime
at leastht
.

the moose

three little
children
eaten by
a moose
sat in its
stomach
trying to
get loose
they tugged
at his tonsils
hollered up
its throat
next thing
they knew
it had
swallowed up
a goat
the goat
butted one
of them
through the
moose's
teeth
when he was
out he
crawled
underneath

tickled moose's
stomach
pulled on its
tail
all of a sudden
they were
swallowed
by a whale
two little
children
inside the
moose
also a goat
and one child
loose
the moose now
was trapped
inside a larger
beast
my oh my
what a whale
of a feast
.

the poet in the well

one time
not so
long ago
when i
was younger
but not so young
i went away

i travelled
over Europe
and ended up
in Spain
living on
a little island
called Ibiza

i rented a
little house
that overlooked
a little bay
with the little
town across
the water

at night
little fishing
boats would
chug to sea
the lights on
their masts
making tracks
across the
darkness

and it was
very beautiful

outside my door
grew a large
fig tree with
ripe and purple
figs to bite and
feel the sweet
thick juices
dribbling down
my chin

there also was
a very young
small lemon
tree which grew
two tiny lemons
that October

yes
it was
very beautiful

the house was
new
it had no
electric lights
yet
it had a pump
for water and
a woodstove for
the cooking

in the kitchen
was a well with
a pump or
a pump with a
well
depending how
you looked at
it and
i was soon to
look at it
both ways

in the front yard
were workmen working
digging a new well
for more water
to put in taps
and it's a good
thing they were
there

for one day
the kitchen well
ran dry so
i took off the
lid
slid down the pipe
and tried to bend
it into the
little bit of
water that was
left
of course it didn't
reach

and then

and then i discovered
i couldn't get out
of the well
the pipe i'd gone down
i couldn't get up
my friend dropped
a rope down but the
well was too narrow
and too deep for me
to pull myself up

so
my friend called
the workmen in
from the front yard
and they laughed
and they laughed
and they pulled
on the rope
and hauled me
up and out of
the well

well

you can imagine
every time after
when i'd meet
them in town
the workmen would
take me into
a bar and buy me
a drink and tell
all their friends
of the crazy
Canadian who got
himself stuck
down a dry Spanish
well

and we'd laugh
and we'd laugh
and we'd laugh
.

the dentist

i used to hate
the dentist
when i was
five or six
and ten
and twelve
and fifteen too
at twenty i'd
get sick
just thinking
of his drill
and stuff
chopping holes
in me
but something
made me
change my
mind
let's see if
you agree

i guess i'd
just turned
twenty-one
or twenty-two
or three
it had been
quite a long
time since
a dentist
had seen
me

one day i
felt a little
ache
somewhere in
my mouth
i think it
was the
north part
rather than
the south
i didn't pay
attention
thought it
would go
away
i went about
my business
and had a
pleasant day

in the evening
it got worse
a little bit
not much
so i took
some aspirin
and now and
then i'd
touch
my face to see
if i could
feel it
hurting any
more
by the time i
went to bed
that night
it was getting
really sore

i lay in bed
i couldn't
sleep
the pain was
getting worse
right from
my tooth up
to my eye
i felt like
i would burst
at ten o'clock
the pain was
bad
eleven it was
awful
by twelve o'clock
i wished that
i was in the
dental hospital
from one to two
to three to four
i rolled and
moaned and
howled
my face was
hot and
swollen and
wrapped up
in a towel

by five o'clock
i thought i'd
die
by six i thought
i had
by seven in
the morning
the pain had
got so bad
i couldn't
see
i couldn't
talk
by eight i
couldn't even
walk
without it
feeling
like my head
was going to
explode
by nine o'clock
i could be seen
running down
the road

i burst into
the dentist's
i leapt into
the chair
i didn't even
look to see
if someone else
was there
i cried
i begged
i pleaded
for him to
ease the pain
i promised not
to stay away
so long ever
again

and so he
pulled my tooth
out
leaving a large gap
right in the front
of my mouth
did i feel like a sap

the pain was
gone
my tooth was
too
for years when
i would talk
to you
i'd be awfully
embarrassed
i'd cover up
my face
until i finally
could afford
a false one
in its place

i sure went
to the dentist
from that time
up to this
and haven't had
such pain again
it's one thing
i don't miss
.

i wish

i wish that
kid would
grow up
he really
makes me
mad
i didn't want
to hit him
and now i feel
real bad
but he is
always teasing
and making
fun of me
and of the
other children
who aren't as
big as he
is
i wish he'd
learn his
lesson

i wonder if
he will
i wish someone
would come
up
with a
niceness pill
i guess we
both could
take it
but he should
take the
most
i'd slip it
in a jar of
jam and spread
it on his
toast
meanwhile
i'll stay away
from him
'cause i don't
want to fight
even though
i'm pretty sure
that i am
in the right.

i wrote on a train

i wrote on
a train as
we rode
through the
rain
a poem full
of choo choos
and rails
and as the
night fell
with the
clang of
the bell
the choo choo
let out a
great wail
the engineer
puffed on
his pipe
and he huffed
that the
rain
was the worst
he had seen

we went
through a
puddle
leaving a
muddle of
feathers
where once
ducks had
been
the night it
got darker
and old
arthur parker
who'd been
this way
often before
said
'something is
up
i'll tell
you
young pup
the rain
it is up
to the
door'

and just as
he said that
we all heard
a great
SPLAT
and looked
out the
windows to
see
a great school
of brown trout
sticking their
tongues out
and then we
saw three
thousand
more
the windows
were leaking
the roof it
was squeaking
the drips were
adropping
on us
when with
a great
sizzle
the engine
did fizzle

and then we
kicked up a great
fuss
'we will not
be fish food
we'll never
be crab bait
we won't let
the watery
horde
know we are
frightened
of spending
the night in
a turtle shell
as room and
board'

the lights
they were
dimming
the fish
they were
swimming
the passengers
huddled
real tight

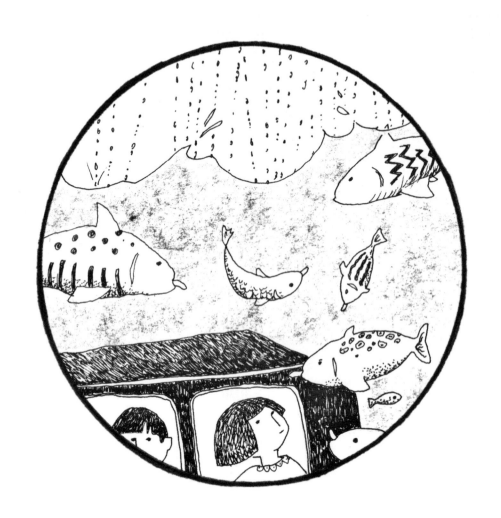

we shivered
and sniffled
and snuffled
and piffled
and prayed
we would get
through
the night
when suddenly
someone
said
'Danny has
some gum
the bubble
kind i do
believe'
so he blew
a great bubble
around our
tight huddle
and opening
the door
we were freed

we popped to
the surface
the fish
bubbling curses
we soon got
picked up
by a boat
the next time
i go on a
train i'll be
certain to
carry a
life saving
float

.

if your name

if your name
starts with
A
on this
(beautiful/rainy/etc.)
day
wave your hand
wave your hand

if your name
starts with
B
touch your knee
i see

if your name
starts with
C
wink at me
wink at me

if your name
starts with
D
make the sound
of a bee
like me

if your name
starts with
E
hop up like
a flea
like a flea

if your name
starts with
F
take a very
deep breath
like this

if your name
starts with
G
pretend your
at sea
row your
boat

if your name
starts with
H
put your hands
on your waist
on your waist

if your name
starts with
I
draw a big
piece of pie
in the air

if your name
starts with
J
point over
that way
that way

if your name
starts with
K
point the other
way
like this

if your name
starts with
L
let out a big
yell
a big
yell

if your name
starts with
M
then you say
amen
like a prayer

if your name
starts with
N
cluck like
a hen
cluck cluck
cluck cluck

if your name
starts with
O
then touch your
elbow
with your nose

if your name
starts with
P
now let me see
you sneeze
you sneeze

if your name
starts with
Q
there aren't
many of you
so stand up
real tall

if your name
starts with
R
honk like
a car
beep beep
beep beep

if your name
starts with
S
then you make
a HISSSSSSSSS
like a snake

if your name
starts with
T
get down on
your knee
on your knee

if your name
starts with
U
then moo
like a cow

if your name
starts with
V
then giggle
with glee
tee hee
tee hee

if your name
starts with
W
you take the
trouble to stand
stand up

if your name
starts with
X
then tickle your
neck
and laugh
and laugh

if your name
starts with
Y
point up to
the sky
very high

if your name
starts with
Z
pat yourself
on the head
on the head

now i know
who you are
and i'll likely
forget
but still i am
very glad that
we met
thank you
thank you
it's been very
nice meeting you
.

my town

on a tall
black tree
sat a
small green
squirrel
its tail was
like a broomstick
its eyes were
all awhirl
and they were blue
so blue
much bluer than
a can of turtle stew

beneath a purple
brick wall
lay an old
yellow cow
and she snored
and she snuffled
and she wheezed
and her eyes were
red in her
fat old head
and she chewed
on a dandelion's
knees

beside a two storied
house lived a
little orange mouse
whose teeth were
tiny and round
but its tail was
as long as a
pink crow's song
and it buried small
piglets in the
ground

in my brother's
left ear
he would always
hear
the call of the
grey horsefly
he would bang
his head
every time he
was fed but
never ever tell
us why

now my family's
odd and so is the
town where i've
lived for most of
my life but
oddest of all is
the twenty foot
tall
polka dotted lady
who's my wife

.

eyeball bouncers

this poem is for
your eyeballs
here's what
they have to
do
they have to
look at something
to the left
of you
now
swing them right
and left again
and do it
five more times
(the trouble with
 this silly poem
 is that it has
 these rhymes)

now
lift your eyes
within your head
to look at something
high
don't move
your head
just eyes instead
(you are allowed
 to sigh)
now
drop them down
look at the
ground
then swing them
up again
and back and
forth and back
and forth
until you've
counted
ten

now
to the left
swing them around
in circles
five times then
go to the right
and swivel them
full circles
up to
ten

you might think
this peculiar
a funny thing
to do
but i've been
told this exercise
is very good
for you
.

Tommy

why did Tommy
push me
why'd he knock
me down
i didn't do
a thing to
him 'cept
say he was
a clown

just 'cause i
laughed and
pointed
and made fun
of his clothes
that wasn't
any reason
to punch me
in the nose

why doesn't
Tommy like me
i think that
he's alright
i want to be
his friend now

(since he beat me
 in the fight)

it really shouldn't
matter that i
joked about his
lunch
and said it
looked like
garbage
why did he have
to punch

just 'cause
i made up
stories
and told them
to the gang
and got them
all to laugh
at him he
didn't have to
bang my head
against the
pavement
and kick me
in the bum

if i asked
him home for
dinner
i wonder if
he'd come
.

i dream

i dream
boy
do i ever
dream
last night
i dreamt that
feathers started
growing
all over my
body

first they grew
on my ears
WOW
did you ever
have feathers
growing
on your ears

well don't

they itch

first
great big
blue ones
grew
they were four
feet long

and then
and then

all around those
great big blue
feathers
little tiny
orange ones
started growing
they weren't
so bad
they were very
soft and very
fluffy
but
they tickled
and if anything's
worse than
an itch
it's a whole
lot of tickle
well

that was bad
enough i
thought

but then
but then

those little
orange feathers
started growing
in my armpits
and if there's
anything that
really tickles
it's feathers
in your armpits

and then
and then

those little
fluffy
tickly
orange feathers
sprouted out
between my
fingers
and my toes
and all down
my legs
and all over
my tummy
and right up
the middle
of my back

OH WOW

did i feel
silly
not to mention
tickly and
also blue itchy
from those
great big blue
feathers
growing on
my ears

suddenly
my hair felt
strange
OH OH
it began to
turn into
white feathers
and grey feathers
and green and yellow
polka dotted
six foot feathers
sticking straight up
in the air

OH WOW

how embarrassing

but then
but then

my eyebrows
sprouted little
fluffy purple
feathers
and all over
my nose grew
little fluffy
red feathers
and my beard
turned into
big long
gold feathers
except my
moustache which
sprouted little
fluffy black
ones and
all the time
they were
tickling and
itching

and then
and then

Pop

with a great
big POP
out of my
belly button
sprouted the
biggest
feather in
the world

i couldn't
believe it

it was nineteen
feet long
it was every
colour you
could imagine
it had
stripes
it had
circles
it had
polka dots
it had
zigs and
it had
zags

and then
and then

it started
to twirl

it went around
once
it went around
twice
it went around
and around
and faster
and faster

and then
and then

those four foot
long blue feathers
growing on my
ears started to
flap
they went faster
and faster
and faster

and then
and then

my body started
to rise off
the bed and get
higher and
higher and
that huge feather
in my belly button
knocked down the
light from
the ceiling
twirled out a
hole in the roof
and flapping from
the ears and
twirling from
the tummy i
rose high into
the midnight
air

and then
and then

those polka dotted
six foot feathers
growing from
my head started
flapping like
crazy and i
began to fly

i flew around
the city
i flew over
the highway
i flew into
the countryside
and over the
forests
i bumped into
nighthawks
collided with
owls
raced past some
geese flying
south
i got to the
ocean
i passed a
jet airplane

i flew over
islands
i flew over
mountains

and then
and then

there below me
my house came
into view

and then
and then

my feathers
started
falling out

first all the
little orange
tickly fluffy
feathers
fell from
my armpits

and from between
my toes and
between my fingers
and off my legs
and off my tummy
and off my back
and off my ears

and then
and then

the white feathers
and the grey feathers
and the green and
yellow polka dotted
six foot feathers
fell from my head
and the four foot
long blue and
itchy feathers
fell from my ears
and all that was
left was the
nineteen foot long
every coloured
feather
twirling in my
belly button

OH WOW

OH NO

OH

THUMP

i fell out
of bed
.

poetry class

ten children
noisy
grouped around
a table
complaining
'oh the pain
of not being
able to rhyme'
they moan
'oh the unfairness
of it all'
'i can't think
of anything
to write'
they sigh
'a rhyme
a rhyme
the world will
end if i can't
rhyme'

meanwhile
quietly
thinking to
themselves
in between
the noisy ones
two or three
good poets
work away filling
up the page
.

school collection

the school is
full of sounds
let's collect
them

i hear
two people
playing ping pong   ping pong

walking down
the hall
i hear
footsteps
left right   left right
                                     ping pong

a door opens
creeeeaaaak   creeeeaaaak
                                     left right
                                     ping pong

a door slams
BANG   BANG
                                     creeeeaaaak
                                     left right
                                     ping pong

the bell rings
riiiiiiing

         riiiiiiing
         BANG
         creeeeaaaak
         left right
         ping pong

a lunch pail
drops
CRASH

         CRASH
         riiiiiiing
         BANG
         creeeeaaaak
         left right
         ping pong

a banana
peels
sliiiiiip

         sliiiiiip
         CRASH
         riiiiiiing
         BANG
         creeeeaaaak
         left right
         ping pong

a phone rings
briiing

briiiiing
sliiiiiiip
CRASH
riiiiiiing
BANG
creeeeaaaak
left right
ping pong

a teacher
shouts
STOP THAT

STOP THAT
briiiiiiing
sliiiiiiiip
CRASH
riiiiiiiing
BANG
creeeeaaaak
left right
ping pong

school's out
HOORAYYYYY

HOORAYYYY

EDUCATION